The Zoo

by

Emily C. Dawson

amicus readers

1

Amicus Readers are published by Amicus
P.O. Box 1329, Mankato, Minnesota 56002

Printed in the United States of America at Corporate Graphics,
North Mankato, Minnesota.

Library of Congress Cataloging-in-Publication Data
Dawson, Emily C.
 The zoo / by Emily C. Dawson.
    p. cm. — (Amicus readers. my community)
 Includes index.
 Summary: "Describes a trip to the zoo in which the reader learns about various animals.
Includes visual literacy activity"—Provided by publisher.
 ISBN 978-1-60753-024-4 (library binding)
 1. Zoos—Juvenile literature. 2. Zoo animals—Juvenile literature. I. Title.
 QL76.D39 2011
 590.7 3—dc22
                        2010011111

Series Editor   Rebecca Glaser
Series Designer   Mary Herrmann
Book Designer   Darren Erickson
Photo Researcher   Heather Dreisbach

Photo Credits
Christopher Furlong/Staff, 1, 15, 21 (giraffe, zookeeper); Harry Walker/photolibrary, cover;
Juniors Bildarchiv/Photolibrary, 9, 20 (gibbon); Kevin Schafer / Alamy, 11, 21 (tortoise);
Maximilian Weinzierl/Alamy, 5; Mira/Alamy, 13, 20 (panda); Neil Cannon/Alamy, 19, 20
(trainer); PETE OXFORD/MINDEN PICTURES/National Geographic Stock, 7, 20 (macaw);
Rosanne Tackaberry / Alamy, 17, 21 (snow monkey)

1223
42010

10 9 8 7 6 5 4 3 2 1

Contents

Today we are going to the zoo. I can't wait to see the snow monkeys.
But first, we visit the birds.

The macaws are loud. They eat fruit and nuts. But they also eat clay to get salt.

I think I see the snow monkeys! But the sign says they are gibbons. Gibbons are apes. They sing loudly in the trees.

Then we see a giant tortoise. It is more than 100 years old. And it's bigger than a kitchen table!

The giant pandas are eating bamboo. They eat for 12 hours a day.

We watch a zookeeper feeding a baby giraffe. It drinks milk from a bottle just like my baby sister.

Finally, we find the snow monkeys. They come from Japan.

We watch an animal show. A sea lion does funny tricks and the animal trainer gives it fish. What a fun day at the zoo!

Picture Glossary

animal trainer—a person who teaches animals to do tricks and perform

giant panda—a black and white bear from Asia

gibbon—a long-armed ape

macaw—a brightly colored, large bird that is related to a parrot

giraffe—an African animal with a very long neck and legs; it has spots on its coat

snow monkey—a monkey from Japan with thick fur that lives easily in cold climates

tortoise—a large turtle that lives on land

zookeeper—a person whose job is taking care of animals at a zoo

The Zoo: A Second Look

Take a second look in the book at the photos to answer these questions.

1. What color is the macaw?

2. How do gibbons and snow monkeys look different?

3. What kind of trick is the sea lion doing?

Check your answers on page 24.

Ideas for Parents and Teachers

My Community, an Amicus Readers Level 1 series, provides essential support for new readers while exploring children's first frame of reference, the community. A picture glossary helps readers connect words and images. The activity page teaches visual literacy and critical thinking skills. Use the following strategies to engage your children or students.

Before Reading
- Read the title and ask the students to suggest animals that might be in this book.
- Have the students talk about trips they've taken to the zoo and what they learned while they were there.
- Look at the picture glossary words. Tell children to watch for them as they read the book.

Read the Book
- "Walk" through the book and look at the photos. Ask the children to guess what kind of animal is on that page.
- Ask the students to read the book independently.
- Provide support where necessary. Show students how to use the picture glossary if they need help with words.

After Reading
- Invite the students to return to the book and talk about the animals they remember from the book. Prompt them with questions, such as *Where do snow monkeys come from? Which animals eat clay?*
- Have the students discuss other animals they have seen while at the zoo that may not have been mentioned in the book.
- Ask the students to make comparisons between the animals in the book and animals they see every day.

INDEX

WEB SITES

Animal Videos, Photos, Facts—National Geographic Kids: http://kids.nationalgeographic.com/

Fort Wayne Children's Zoo: http://www.kidszoo.org

San Diego Zoo Kids' Territory: http://www.sandiegozoo.org/kids/index.html

Smithsonian National Zoo: http://nationalzoo.si.edu/Animals/

ANSWERS FROM PAGE 22

1. Blue and yellow

2. Gibbons have brown and white fur, and snow monkeys have white fur. Snow monkeys have no hair on their faces and gibbons do.

3. Jumping through a Hula-hoop.